MW01129380

 # SIGHT WORDS

THIS BOOK BELONGS TO

_____

- -

_____

SCHOLASTIC PANDA EDUCATION

ISBN: 978-1-953149-29-9

Copyright © 2020 by Scholastic Panda Education
Second Paperback Edition: September 2020
First Paperback Edition: May 2019

SIGHT WORD SET 1

☆ Read and trace ☆

the   of   and

☆ ☆ Color it ☆ ☆

the   of   and

☆ Circle them ☆

the
of
and

the   be   green   of   and   an

not   of

blue   and   it   the   all   red

☆ ☆ Spell it ☆ ☆

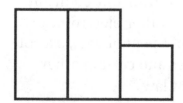 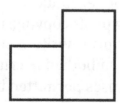 

☆ **Put it in a sentence** ☆

I see _____ cat.

It is black _____ blue.

I got out _____ bed.

WORDS

and
of
the
And
Of
The

☆ ☆ **Find them** ☆ ☆

O	X	O	S	i	s	Y	R
q	K	D	K	T	f	g	l
A	y	O	X	u	n	O	s
J	u	o	b	T	w	o	f
I	O	N	W	l	h	b	Q
v	w	R	A	n	d	e	N
m	D	s	Z	n	h	W	X
h	I	X	a	t	g	y	W

the   of   and

_____   _____   _____

_____   _____   _____

_____   _____   _____

_____   _____   _____

SIGHT WORD SET 2

☆ Read and trace ☆

a   to   in

☆ ☆ Color it ☆ ☆

a   to   in

☆ Circle them ☆

a
to
in

in   be   was   in   and   a   red

to   car   a   new   it   pink   to   orange

☆ ☆ Spell it ☆ ☆

☆ **Put it in a sentence** ☆

I ate _____ snack.

It belongs _____ me.

I live _____ New York.

<u>WORDS</u>   ☆ ☆ **Find them** ☆ ☆

a
to
in
A
To
In

R	J	J	Y	i	o	n	A
t	N	c	U	O	D	h	Z
n	U	s	h	i	y	X	g
F	v	B	Q	M	c	o	H
V	Z	Q	V	k	g	l	d
t	M	x	j	P	l	G	T
I	D	C	c	M	n	t	o
k	D	L	t	k	a	i	n

a   to   in

SIGHT WORD SET 3

☆ Read and trace ☆

is   you   that

☆ ☆ Color it ☆ ☆

is   you   that

☆ Circle them ☆

| is |
| you |
| that |

is   be   night   they   is   you
them   that   you   boat
red   it   house   to   that

☆ ☆ Spell it ☆ ☆

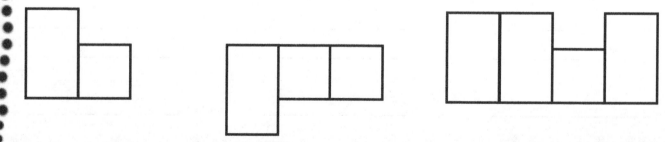

It _____ big.

_____ did great!

_____ is yours.

WORDS   ☆ ☆ **Find them** ☆ ☆

is
you
that
Is
You
That

b	W	b	x	E	C	O	i
B	k	Y	d	D	P	E	s
a	h	u	x	g	I	I	U
h	Y	o	u	X	l	o	k
k	T	o	p	J	a	v	k
Z	y	h	y	J	d	A	z
e	N	X	a	k	s	P	o
S	w	L	r	t	h	a	t

is   you   that

_____   _____   _____

SIGHT WORD SET 4

☆ Read and trace ☆

it   he   for

☆ ☆ Color it ☆ ☆

it   he   for

☆ Circle them ☆

it
he
for

for   me   he   am   he   she

them   that   you   it

brown   it   duck   to   for

☆ ☆ Spell it ☆ ☆

☆ **Put it in a sentence** ☆

I like _____ .

_____ is my friend.

The candy was _____ you.

__WORDS__   ☆ ☆ **Find them** ☆ ☆

it
he
for
It
He
For

y	s	B	J	o	u	i	l
A	o	Y	a	f	F	H	t
c	t	Z	f	o	z	a	z
W	n	P	W	o	L	s	q
F	U	f	r	o	N	V	y
d	o	o	P	a	R	P	A
Y	x	r	k	d	q	l	h
I	G	k	L	h	i	H	e

it

he

for

SIGHT WORD SET 5

☆ **Read and trace** ☆

was   on   are

☆ ☆ **Color it** ☆ ☆

was   on   are

☆ **Circle them** ☆

was
on
are

on   was   are   am   he   on
cat   this   you   quick
fox   it   was   in   are

☆ ☆ **Spell it** ☆ ☆

☆ **Put it in a sentence** ☆

_____ that you?

It is _____ the table.

They _____ your books.

<u>WORDS</u>   ☆ ☆ **Find them** ☆ ☆

was
on
are
Was
On
Are

b	V	w	d	Z	r	C	j
d	G	Q	I	O	W	i	v
Z	E	F	c	q	i	a	j
N	l	v	j	G	j	r	s
R	E	I	U	A	r	e	Z
E	O	o	x	b	w	c	w
K	B	n	K	C	l	Y	a
I	g	x	R	O	B	l	s

Was   on   are

_____   _____   _____

SIGHT WORD SET 6

☆ Read and trace ☆

☆ ☆ Color it ☆ ☆

as not but

☆ Circle them ☆

as
not
but

not   is   but   I   he   but

dog   where   you   not

as   it   as   door   us

☆ ☆ Spell it ☆ ☆

 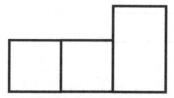 

Quiet _____ a mouse.

It is hot _____ cold.

It is cloudy _____ warm.

WORDS

as
not
but
As
Not
But

☆ ☆ Find them ☆ ☆

n	o	t	F	b	G	Z	g
B	u	t	a	L	n	c	N
b	m	A	s	p	T	N	y
f	t	Z	H	o	J	A	m
B	T	e	w	r	f	M	A
I	t	N	b	U	T	I	H
i	M	o	U	w	B	Q	m
c	v	t	f	B	D	U	m

as

not

but

SIGHT WORD SET 7

☆ Read and trace ☆

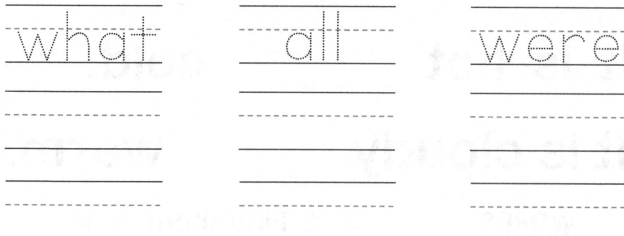

what   all   were

☆ ☆ Color it ☆ ☆

what all were

☆ Circle them ☆

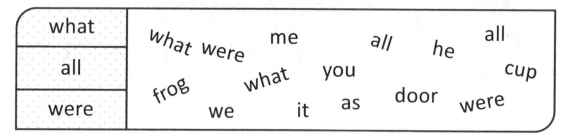

what
all
were

what were   me   all   he   all
frog   we what you   cup
we   it as door were

☆ ☆ Spell it ☆ ☆

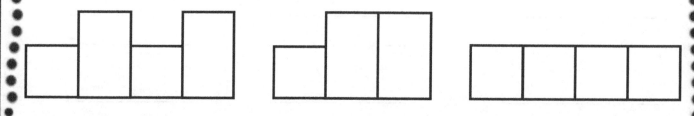

_____
- - - - - - - - -   is that?
_____

Is that   _____   ?
- - - - - - - - -
_____

Yes, they   _____   there.
- - - - - - - - -
_____

<u>WORDS</u>   ☆ ☆ **Find them** ☆ ☆

what

all

were

What

All

Were

S	X	E	q	J	m	p	i
V	y	A	E	W	A	W	H
c	W	X	I	t	S	C	S
w	y	C	a	l	l	Q	Q
T	W	h	a	t	Q	k	G
u	w	e	r	e	C	F	y
V	P	M	r	m	x	h	k
e	E	M	A	e	n	o	y

what   all   were

_____   _____   _____
- - - - - - -   - - - - - - -   - - - - - - -
_____   _____   _____

_____   _____   _____

_____   _____   _____

SIGHT WORD SET 8

☆ Read and trace ☆

when   we   there

☆ ☆ Color it ☆ ☆

when we there

☆ Circle them ☆

when
we
there

when   were   who   we   cow   when

there   will   you   cup

we   there   as   door   there

☆ ☆ Spell it ☆ ☆

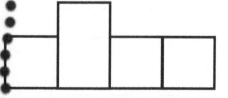  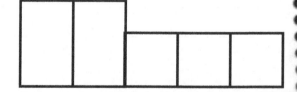

☆ **Put it in a sentence** ☆

_____ did he leave?

Can _____ go?

Look over _____ .

WORDS   ☆ ☆ **Find them** ☆ ☆

when
we
there
When
We
There

t	p	d	l	q	o	l	V
h	T	I	F	Q	W	e	P
e	i	V	o	v	T	Y	j
r	y	w	e	T	J	l	W
e	g	c	h	h	n	l	r
e	P	J	W	e	k	z	z
Y	M	x	h	r	n	T	Z
C	j	W	v	e	l	b	G

when   we   there

SIGHT WORD SET 9

☆ **Read and trace** ☆

can   an   your

☆ ☆ **Color it** ☆ ☆

can   an   your

☆ **Circle them** ☆

can	
an	
your	

too   your   an   clock   cow   can

down   can   fox   milk

circle   your   up   apple   an

☆ ☆ **Spell it** ☆ ☆

_____ you hear that?

Is that _____ apple?

Please eat _____ food.

WORDS

☆ ☆ **Find them** ☆ ☆

can

an

your

Can

An

Your

U	f	l	P	z	k	y	b
F	U	X	o	h	H	o	M
z	d	M	R	P	M	u	H
f	H	q	J	x	P	r	i
Q	n	Y	N	c	u	u	J
c	t	V	D	o	a	A	y
p	a	O	Y	C	a	n	y
J	b	Z	O	P	a	q	F

can

an

your

SIGHT WORD SET 10

☆ Read and trace ☆

which   their   said

☆ ☆ Color it ☆ ☆

which their said

☆ Circle them ☆

which
their
said

two   blue   us   which   green   said

down   their   pig   three

which   mine   left   their   said

☆ ☆ Spell it ☆ ☆

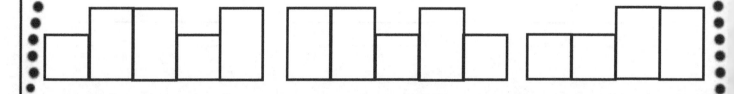

Say _____ one you want.

_____ cat ran away.

He _____ thank you.

WORDS

☆ ☆ **Find them** ☆ ☆

which
their
said
Which
Their
Said

f	R	W	q	z	P	I	J
z	t	M	h	Q	d	W	A
h	T	h	e	i	r	h	A
V	o	S	e	W	c	g	i
Q	P	s	a	i	d	h	d
D	g	X	h	i	r	z	B
R	U	w	T	x	d	m	J
Y	d	t	J	E	i	B	h

which

their

said

SIGHT WORD SET 11

☆ Read and trace ☆

if   do   into

☆ ☆ Color it ☆ ☆

if   do   into

☆ Circle them ☆

if
do
into

four   if   nine   bee   color   if
do   their   into   how
into   dish   right   their   do

☆ ☆ Spell it ☆ ☆

_____
- - - - - - - - - - - - - -
_____ we were older.
_____
- - - - - - - - - - - - - -
_____ you like fish?
_____
Go - - - - - - - - - - - - - - the water.
_____

<u>WORDS</u>   ☆ ☆ **Find them** ☆ ☆

```
if
do
into
If
Do
Into
```

U	d	e	l	H	N	a	v
n	C	v	j	n	d	o	L
Z	q	Q	C	c	t	D	j
e	s	z	F	n	R	o	q
k	j	i	i	f	z	p	w
J	J	B	l	P	s	r	p
n	e	s	i	N	f	H	f
v	l	j	G	r	E	G	w

if

do

into

SIGHT WORD SET 12

☆ **Read and trace** ☆

has   more   her

☆ ☆ **Color it** ☆ ☆

has   more   her

☆ **Circle them** ☆

| has |
| more |
| her |

sell   has   her   bee   rain   has
more   from   more   their   who
new   pink   right   her

☆ ☆ **Spell it** ☆ ☆

☆ **Put it in a sentence** ☆

She _____ **it.**

One _____ **time.**

Let's find _____ **.**

<u>WORDS</u>

☆ ☆ **Find them** ☆ ☆

has
more
her
Has
More
Her

g	s	o	z	l	w	o	y
x	o	j	Q	T	v	T	X
M	m	C	E	W	H	T	w
x	o	b	Y	K	z	o	C
B	r	r	n	j	V	D	K
G	e	H	e	h	A	y	E
h	x	e	a	a	P	o	p
K	j	r	J	s	J	O	p

has   more   her

SIGHT WORD SET 13

☆ Read and trace ☆

two   like   him

☆ ☆ Color it ☆ ☆

two   like   him

☆ Circle them ☆

two
like
him

pen   went   mom   two   him   like

like   eight   more   we   two

drop   him   table   dad

☆ ☆ Spell it ☆ ☆

Can I have _____ please?

I _____ ice cream.

I saw _____ today.

WORDS   ☆ ☆ Find them ☆ ☆

two
like
him
Two
Like
Him

l	V	k	l	i	W	L	R
i	k	l	g	M	Q	j	d
S	a	M	V	e	l	E	e
D	h	a	k	o	J	D	U
D	L	i	k	e	t	N	i
B	l	Z	m	T	w	o	T
j	w	i	e	d	o	e	r
O	H	K	D	e	W	I	Z

two   like   him

SIGHT WORD SET 14

☆ Read and trace ☆

see   time   could

☆ ☆ Color it ☆ ☆

see   time   could

☆ Circle them ☆

see
time
could

could   see   baby   water   paper   time

bird   one   could   fire   lid

time   six   chair   see

☆ ☆ Spell it ☆ ☆

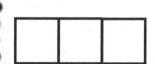 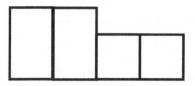 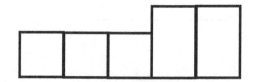

☆ **Put it in a sentence** ☆

Do you _____ that?

It is _____ to go.

I wish I _____ go too.

<u>WORDS</u>   ☆ ☆ **Find them** ☆ ☆

see
time
could
See
Time
Could

l	c	H	C	x	t	Q	F
h	a	m	c	o	u	l	d
e	A	T	x	S	u	q	M
o	u	u	i	a	e	l	B
f	E	h	k	m	n	e	d
o	M	x	i	Z	e	o	E
m	s	t	o	s	k	m	E
p	T	f	D	Z	f	c	P

see

time

could

SIGHT WORD SET 15

☆ **Read and trace** ☆

no   make   than

☆ ☆ **Color it** ☆ ☆

no   make   than

☆ **Circle them** ☆

no
make
than

than   no   child   water   paper   than

grass   warm   make   ice   key

make   glass   black   no

☆ ☆ **Spell it** ☆ ☆

There is _____ time left.

Who will _____ it?

She is taller _____ him.

WORDS

☆ ☆ **Find them** ☆ ☆

no
make
than
No
Make
Than

r	s	l	f	p	q	V	W
P	s	V	i	t	T	Y	u
g	K	f	l	c	h	m	W
s	a	U	r	O	a	a	e
R	F	P	t	K	n	k	n
b	k	f	M	P	a	e	o
w	e	l	S	M	t	N	F
Q	b	d	K	k	P	R	s

no   make   than

SIGHT WORD SET 16

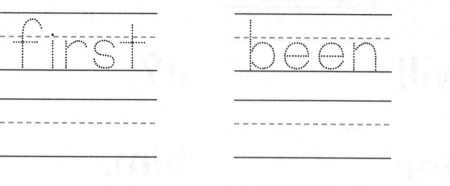
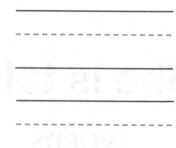

☆ ☆ **Color it** ☆ ☆

☆ **Circle them** ☆

first
been
its

clean   its   proud   water   pencil   first

stick   cool   first   been   top

been   eyes   red   its

☆ ☆ **Spell it** ☆ ☆

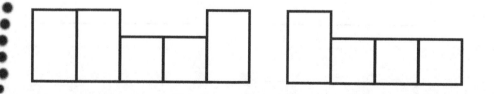

☆ Put it in a sentence ☆

May I go _____ ?

It has _____ a long time.

_____ name is Rex.

WORDS   ☆ ☆ Find them ☆ ☆

first
been
its
First
Been
Its

f	i	r	s	t	b	l	g
l	t	s	s	Z	e	Z	u
O	s	r	B	e	e	n	C
v	i	P	C	s	n	I	K
F	s	d	n	p	w	r	w
j	J	h	D	b	D	Z	h
d	G	o	l	m	O	K	J
E	o	E	v	r	Y	f	d

first

been

its

SIGHT WORD SET 17

water   long   little

☆ ☆ **Color it** ☆ ☆

water   long   little

☆ **Circle them** ☆

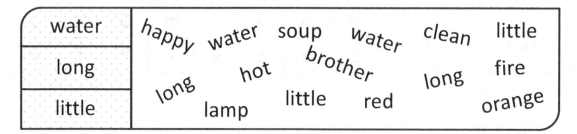

water
long
little

happy   water   soup   water   clean   little
long   hot   brother   long   fire
lamp   little   red   orange

☆ ☆ **Spell it** ☆ ☆

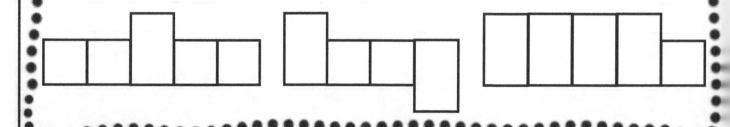

☆ Put it in a sentence ☆

The _____ is cold.

This is a _____ book.

I like this one a _____ .

WORDS

water
long
little
Water
Long
Little

☆ ☆ Find them ☆ ☆

l	o	n	g	g	H	e	F
i	v	W	n	J	r	U	q
t	O	o	v	e	i	E	n
t	L	i	t	t	l	e	A
l	W	a	t	e	r	u	R
e	w	l	E	l	a	u	w
F	t	K	H	l	a	k	z
X	s	d	E	P	z	N	j

water

long

little

SIGHT WORD SET 18

☆ Read and trace ☆

very   after   words

☆ ☆ Color it ☆ ☆

very after words

☆ Circle them ☆

very
after
words

words   very   think   water   nose   very

see   plate   words   long   fork

after   line   spell   after

☆ ☆ Spell it ☆ ☆

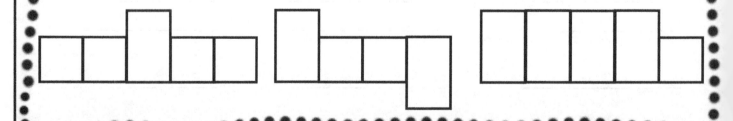

The road is _____ long.

Call _____ 6 PM, please.

How many _____ are there?

WORDS

☆ ☆ **Find them** ☆ ☆

very
after
words
Very
After
Words

z	M	W	R	t	o	s	s
O	g	w	o	r	d	s	g
A	f	t	e	r	v	d	C
z	x	t	o	k	e	E	e
T	f	W	N	o	r	x	s
a	z	V	e	r	y	v	L
i	k	U	i	q	Y	J	D
u	a	Y	L	u	m	r	D

very

after

words

SIGHT WORD SET 19

☆ **Read and trace** ☆

called   just   where

☆ ☆ **Color it** ☆ ☆

called just where

☆ **Circle them** ☆

called
just
where

words   cow   called   hello   cereal   called
where   just   help   just   bat
line   tree   pet   where

☆ ☆ **Spell it** ☆ ☆

☆ **Put it in a sentence** ☆

She _____ for you.

He came in _____ now.

_____ have you been?

WORDS

☆ ☆ **Find them** ☆ ☆

called
just
where
Called
Just
Where

O	I	K	l	k	J	m	S
C	T	K	B	k	H	z	g
W	a	M	j	o	c	v	Z
O	h	l	m	I	D	A	y
K	O	e	l	j	m	J	m
w	h	e	r	e	u	u	E
c	a	l	l	e	d	s	X
x	p	H	G	c	Z	t	t

called

just

where

SIGHT WORD SET 20

☆ Read and trace ☆

most   know   get

☆ ☆ Color it ☆ ☆

most know get

☆ Circle them ☆

most
know
get

like   most   get   give   play   most

know   try   know   gold   run

know   circle   tell   pet   get

☆ ☆ Spell it ☆ ☆

_____ of the animals are cute.

Do you _____ how to read?

Come and _____ it.

WORDS

☆ ☆ **Find them** ☆ ☆

most
know
get
Most
Know
Get

M	o	s	t	i	H	s	H
O	G	e	t	H	E	n	y
t	g	m	m	G	b	f	h
m	S	D	K	D	S	l	k
p	e	S	Q	n	Y	F	h
S	P	R	n	W	o	f	u
b	u	U	k	n	o	w	w
g	m	o	s	t	G	C	H

most

know

get

SIGHT WORD SET 21

☆ Read and trace ☆

through   back   much

☆ ☆ Color it ☆ ☆

through back much

☆ Circle them ☆

through
back
much

back   all   through   give   play   back

free   try   much   through   run

much   tell   pet   get

☆ ☆ Spell it ☆ ☆

☆ **Put it in a sentence** ☆

Go _____ the door.

Give it _____ .

How _____ is it?

WORDS ☆ ☆ **Find them** ☆ ☆

through
back
much
Through
Back
Much

e	Q	Q	M	G	C	h	C
c	f	g	m	e	g	Q	C
H	e	L	p	u	R	h	m
p	q	z	o	a	c	b	B
t	h	r	o	u	g	h	a
s	h	Q	M	O	u	Y	c
T	b	a	c	k	D	k	k
C	T	A	r	B	f	t	F

through   back   much

SIGHT WORD SET 22

☆ Read and trace ☆

before   think   also

☆ ☆ Color it ☆ ☆

before think also

☆ Circle them ☆

before
think
also

also   me   before   rope   play   also

think   too   think   now   walk

much   yes   blue   later

☆ ☆ Spell it ☆ ☆

Please arrive _____ **7 PM.**

I _____ **I saw I her.**

He _____ **plays sports.**

WORDS   ☆ ☆ **Find them** ☆ ☆

before
think
also
Before
Think
Also

a	S	b	A	V	X	T	T
b	I	S	I	H	e	t	d
T	G	s	s	r	e	x	E
B	e	f	o	r	e	l	k
V	O	f	O	m	H	D	y
c	e	T	h	i	n	k	g
b	z	q	I	s	I	L	O
I	t	h	i	n	k	H	h

before   think   also

SIGHT WORD SET 23

☆ **Read and trace** ☆

around   another   came

☆ ☆ **Color it** ☆ ☆

around another came

☆ **Circle them** ☆

around
another
came

also another around spoke came new
true came hope before talk
such another color around

☆ ☆ **Spell it** ☆ ☆

_____ the world.

That's _____ great song.

We _____ home today.

<u>WORDS</u>   ☆ ☆ **Find them** ☆ ☆

```
around
another
came
Around
Another
Came
```

m	x	s	l	P	Q	a	e
A	n	o	t	h	e	r	A
r	W	C	a	m	e	o	d
o	f	V	a	h	v	u	s
u	W	c	t	H	x	n	v
n	X	o	e	d	c	d	m
d	n	V	B	h	O	l	L
a	d	x	x	a	p	i	q

around   another   came

_____   _____   _____

SIGHT WORD SET 24

☆ Read and trace ☆

come   work   three

☆ ☆ Color it ☆ ☆

come   work   three

☆ Circle them ☆

come
work
three

back come three   get came three

much little   just   come where

think work know work

☆ ☆ Spell it ☆ ☆

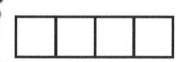 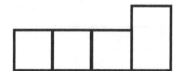 

☆ Put it in a sentence ☆

_____ with us.

I am at _____ now.

There are _____ toys.

WORDS

☆ ☆ **Find them** ☆ ☆

come
work
three
Come
Work
Three

y	E	S	u	v	j	t	D
H	J	S	H	U	Q	x	A
T	s	e	y	Z	d	u	f
C	h	Q	u	y	o	F	c
w	o	r	X	V	C	D	n
c	o	m	e	w	a	y	p
t	h	r	e	e	e	F	b
W	o	r	k	w	o	X	o

come _____

work _____

three _____

SIGHT WORD SET 25

☆ Read and trace ☆

word   must   because

☆ ☆ Color it ☆ ☆

word   must   because

☆ Circle them ☆

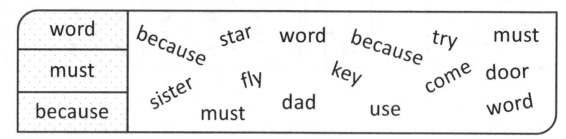

word
must
because

because   star   word   because   try   must

sister   fly   key   come   door

must   dad   use   word

☆ ☆ Spell it ☆ ☆

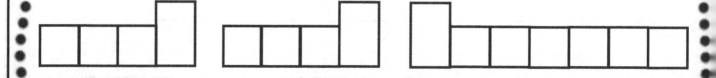

Read the _____ out loud.

I _____ get a haircut.

I like math _____ it's fun!

WORDS   ☆ ☆ **Find them** ☆ ☆

word
must
because
Word
Must
Because

B	L	C	d	k	j	M	N
W	e	r	t	r	t	u	b
Z	o	c	j	x	V	s	H
w	j	r	a	Y	s	t	b
I	o	L	d	u	s	Y	I
b	e	c	a	u	s	e	N
m	h	c	m	L	u	e	f
Z	G	h	I	R	X	G	I

word   must   because

_____   _____   _____

SIGHT WORD SET 26

☆ Read and trace ☆

does   part   even

☆ ☆ Color it ☆ ☆

does   part   even

☆ Circle them ☆

does
part
even

free   does   word   get   my   part
even   true   truth   come   two
way   part   does   even

☆ ☆ Spell it ☆ ☆

_____ that make sense?

I ate _____ of it.

Number two is _____ .

WORDS　　　　☆ ☆ **Find them** ☆ ☆

does
part
even
Does
Part
Even

V	w	G	N	E	K	A	c
Q	w	o	D	U	u	a	i
e	i	R	P	o	S	n	u
y	d	Q	E	a	e	t	B
t	J	o	H	v	r	s	g
M	s	T	e	a	e	t	v
p	Q	C	p	s	C	n	U
o	C	x	E	a	N	a	U

does　　　　　part　　　　　even

SIGHT WORD SET 27

☆ Read and trace ☆

place   well   with

☆ ☆ Color it ☆ ☆

place   well   with

☆ Circle them ☆

place
well
with

new   place   eyes   well   nine   with

bird   well   truth   place   six

with   fish   could   odd

☆ ☆ Spell it ☆ ☆

What's the name of this _____ ?

I am doing _____ .

Can I go _____ you?

WORDS

☆ ☆ Find them ☆ ☆

place
well
with
Place
Well
With

W	P	I	o	Q	I	N	D
w	e	l	l	X	u	t	i
i	B	l	a	W	e	Z	d
t	U	M	l	c	i	D	M
h	G	l	a	f	e	t	G
e	b	l	u	U	E	K	h
s	p	Y	B	d	K	q	t
u	f	w	t	B	R	b	D

place

well

with

SIGHT WORD SET 28

☆ **Read and trace** ☆

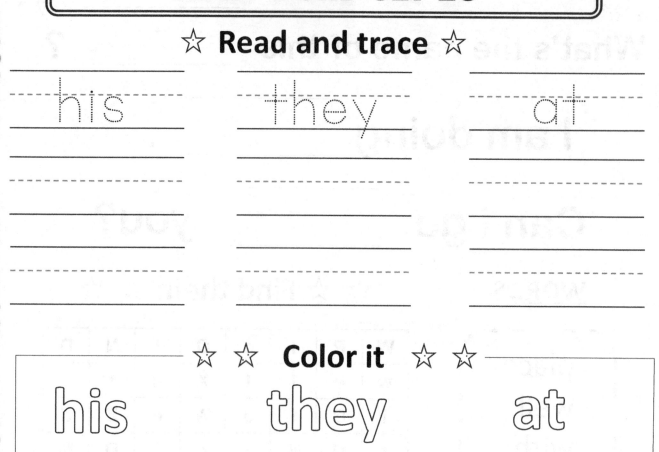

☆ ☆ **Color it** ☆ ☆

his   they   at

☆ **Circle them** ☆

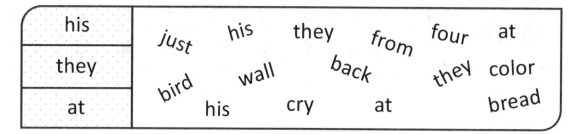

his
they
at

just   his   they   from   four   at

bird   wall   back   they   color

his   cry   at   bread

☆ ☆ **Spell it** ☆ ☆

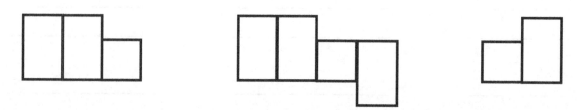

☆ Put it in a sentence ☆

The car is _____ .

Are _____ new here?

It starts _____ 10 AM.

WORDS

his
they
at
His
They
At

☆ ☆ Find them ☆ ☆

C	a	Q	H	E	U	U	y
S	t	x	I	v	V	O	B
k	n	p	I	A	H	u	R
t	X	J	v	M	t	i	F
j	P	m	N	a	h	i	s
R	C	w	V	z	e	s	v
t	m	T	h	e	y	s	d
h	q	r	K	C	G	z	K

his

they

at

SIGHT WORD SET 29

☆ **Read and trace** ☆

be   this   from

☆ ☆ **Color it** ☆ ☆

be   this   from

☆ **Circle them** ☆

be
this
from

bee   be   while   from   flour   west

flower   water   be   they   this

this   from   snake   tooth

☆ ☆ **Spell it** ☆ ☆

Try to _____ very quiet.

I like _____ one a lot!

Where are you _____ ?

WORDS

☆ ☆ **Find them** ☆ ☆

be
this
from
Be
This
From

o	M	x	o	s	O	B	b
H	s	X	c	F	s	n	e
i	P	a	i	J	Y	J	Y
H	X	L	f	U	D	y	r
F	q	S	f	T	e	P	t
w	r	W	d	D	h	q	h
c	f	o	w	x	u	i	i
f	r	o	m	G	o	w	s

be

this

from

SIGHT WORD SET 30

☆ Read and trace ☆

I   have   or

☆ ☆ Color it ☆ ☆

I   have   or

☆ Circle them ☆

I
have
or

bee   be   while   from   flour   west

flower   water   be   they   this

this   from   snake   tooth

☆ ☆ Spell it ☆ ☆

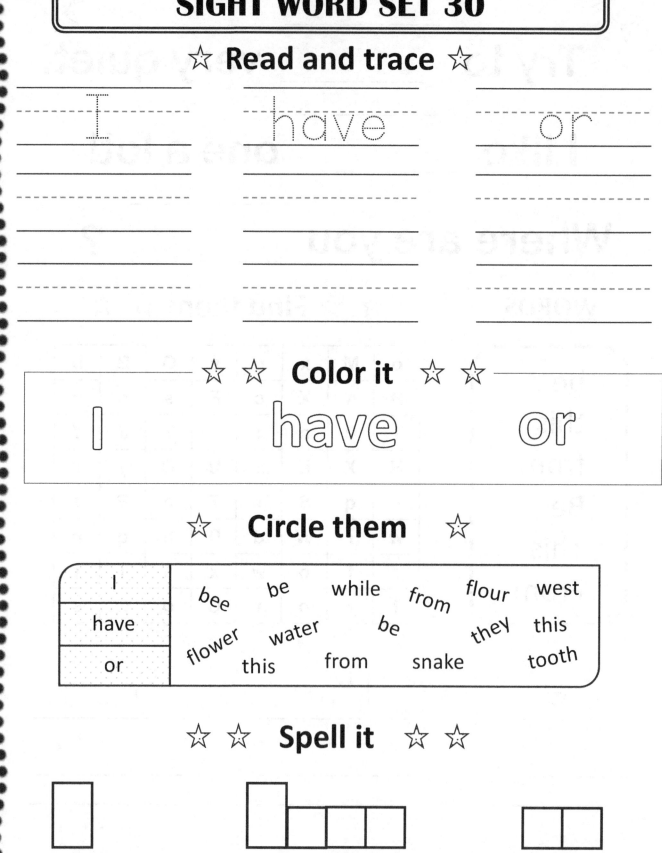

☆ Put it in a sentence ☆

_____ am happy.

I _____ many friends!

Do you want this _____ that?

WORDS

I
have
or
Have
Or

☆ ☆ **Find them** ☆ ☆

H	W	t	S	M	D	e	G
t	a	z	e	L	a	G	k
o	E	v	Y	M	h	O	E
Y	a	V	e	g	a	Q	r
h	G	G	N	Q	v	o	C
G	R	X	B	d	C	I	H
M	w	j	X	W	p	H	m
t	f	z	a	L	X	Y	s

I   have   or

SIGHT WORD SET 31

☆ Read and trace ☆

by   one   had

☆ ☆ Color it ☆ ☆

by   one   had

☆ Circle them ☆

by
one
had

never by speak snow one shoe

stripe had   by   now most

one drive snake had

☆ ☆ Spell it ☆ ☆

☆ **Put it in a sentence** ☆

I don't like to play _____ myself.

Is this a good _____ ?

I _____ so much fun!

WORDS   ☆ ☆ **Find them** ☆ ☆

by
one
had
By
One
Had

O	n	e	u	b	M	i	J
o	n	j	e	V	c	p	H
o	B	k	C	X	E	w	d
H	S	H	W	R	X	j	m
K	K	L	a	q	z	h	R
n	Q	a	c	d	z	B	b
h	Z	E	a	W	g	F	y
H	K	h	E	n	j	i	u

by   one   had

SIGHT WORD SET 32

☆ **Read and trace** ☆

will   each   about

☆ ☆ **Color it** ☆ ☆

will   each   about

☆ **Circle them** ☆

will
each
about

forever   sun   each   rain   one   black

each   had   top   about   most

about   will   grass   will

☆ ☆ **Spell it** ☆ ☆

☆ **Put it in a sentence** ☆

_____ you help me?

_____ of us is important.

What is the movie _____ ?

WORDS   ☆ ☆ **Find them** ☆ ☆

will
each
about
Will
Each
About

a	c	s	u	r	U	v	A
b	O	h	R	Z	d	o	B
o	M	X	M	h	w	d	n
u	E	a	c	h	D	X	B
t	t	a	l	J	n	F	I
f	e	l	A	D	j	U	y
W	i	l	l	b	p	t	b
w	D	D	A	b	o	u	t

will   each   about

_____   _____   _____

SIGHT WORD SET 33

☆ Read and trace ☆

how   up   out

☆ ☆ Color it ☆ ☆

how up out

☆ Circle them ☆

how
up
out

day out each dark trash how

fur how night out most

learn up glass up

☆ ☆ Spell it ☆ ☆

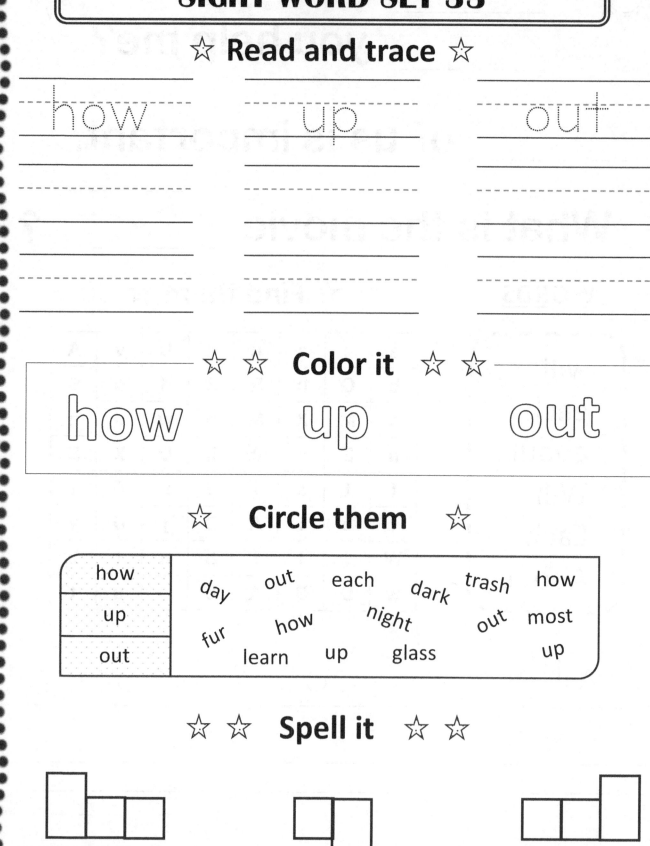

☆ **Put it in a sentence** ☆

_____
- - - - - - - - - - -   **did you do that?**
_____

It is _____ **to you.**

I will find _____ .

WORDS   ☆ ☆ **Find them** ☆ ☆

how
up
out
How
Up
Out

e	L	n	R	R	z	k	E
V	R	f	c	d	L	g	M
x	C	E	m	Y	h	x	H
v	E	J	M	O	r	o	o
T	I	J	O	U	u	u	w
m	w	d	f	O	p	t	d
r	u	y	k	B	C	O	o
i	C	m	k	G	Y	k	g

how

up

out

SIGHT WORD SET 34

them   then   she

☆ ☆ **Color it** ☆ ☆

them   then   she

☆ **Circle them** ☆

them
then
she

clean   then   water   them   then   made

fun   she   night   out   why

them   up   glass   she

☆ ☆ **Spell it** ☆ ☆

☆ **Put it in a sentence** ☆

Do you know _____ ?

Will I see you before _____ ?

_____ is amazing!

WORDS

☆ ☆ **Find them** ☆ ☆

them
then
she
Them
Then
She

a	H	p	M	Q	c	y	T
o	U	T	B	p	P	I	M
D	C	r	s	F	X	p	B
I	g	P	T	h	e	n	W
w	Y	H	t	h	e	m	x
y	P	P	S	h	e	L	H
r	l	a	t	f	F	m	W
J	W	N	u	i	s	Z	C

them

then

she

SIGHT WORD SET 35

many   some   so

☆ ☆ **Color it** ☆ ☆

many   some   so

☆ **Circle them** ☆

many
some
so

dirt   many   time   so   power   some

so   as   night   many   would

them   some   worm   mouse

☆ ☆ **Spell it** ☆ ☆

There are _____ turtles.

There is _____ for her.

This apple is _____ tasty!

WORDS

☆ ☆ **Find them** ☆ ☆

many
some
so
Many
Some
So

m	a	n	y	S	o	m	e
m	e	n	p	s	o	m	n
A	a	V	k	X	o	s	q
M	s	N	Q	s	u	Y	P
x	Y	e	y	F	i	v	N
O	E	N	Z	S	d	X	g
j	o	T	L	I	D	i	e
V	a	r	m	U	r	B	t

many

some

so

SIGHT WORD SET 36

☆ Read and trace ☆

these would who

☆ ☆ Color it ☆ ☆

these would who

☆ Circle them ☆

these
would
who

then these wheel old look who

button down would many would

who some these proud

☆ ☆ Spell it ☆ ☆

_____ are very special.

_____ you like to go?

_____ makes you happy?

WORDS   ☆ ☆ **Find them** ☆ ☆

these
would
who
These
Would
Who

p	t	z	h	o	u	Y	w
J	f	H	h	k	G	U	w
E	W	V	g	d	W	h	o
I	K	i	A	p	e	h	u
m	e	S	s	s	w	M	l
q	J	i	e	R	r	W	d
n	t	h	e	s	e	P	v
x	T	u	W	o	u	l	d

these   would   who

SIGHT WORD SET 37

☆ **Read and trace** ☆

now   people   my

☆ ☆ **Color it** ☆ ☆

now   people   my

☆ **Circle them** ☆

now
people
my

fall   help   my   you   look   now

use   now   people   so   would

people   hear   too   my

☆ ☆ **Spell it** ☆ ☆

☆ **Put it in a sentence** ☆

Are you ready _____ ?

There are _____ everywhere.

That's _____ mom and dad.

WORDS

☆ ☆ **Find them** ☆ ☆

now
people
my
Now
People
My

u	c	x	m	y	c	w	m
P	e	s	M	D	H	L	j
P	e	n	j	j	e	Q	f
R	D	o	t	l	h	Y	k
l	a	w	p	R	Q	I	N
R	o	o	h	l	l	t	e
N	e	k	R	s	e	q	K
p	X	x	V	i	N	g	S

now

people

my

SIGHT WORD SET 38

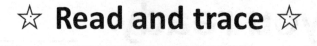

☆ **Read and trace** ☆

made   over   did

☆ ☆ **Color it** ☆ ☆

made over did

☆ **Circle them** ☆

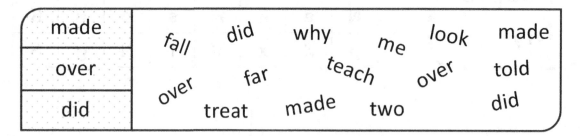

| made |
| over |
| did |

fall   did   why   me   look   made

over   far   teach   over   told

treat   made   two   did

☆ ☆ **Spell it** ☆ ☆

 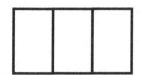

I _____ a cake for you.

The game is _____ .

Look at what I _____ !

WORDS ☆ ☆ **Find them** ☆ ☆

made
over
did
Made
Over
Did

V	f	I	J	L	I	T	Q
v	R	U	v	O	G	J	o
t	A	D	V	M	v	x	v
w	z	q	i	F	a	e	e
H	M	D	p	d	i	d	r
f	N	n	h	l	a	k	e
o	u	t	z	m	f	p	r
C	G	L	x	p	U	S	p

made

over

did

SIGHT WORD SET 39

☆ **Read and trace** ☆

down   only   way

☆ ☆ **Color it** ☆ ☆

down   only   way

☆ **Circle them** ☆

down
only
way

fall down why way look only

way far teach down told

only made two did

☆ ☆ **Spell it** ☆ ☆

Don't look _____ !

This is the _____ choice.

I will show you the _____ .

WORDS   ☆ ☆ **Find them** ☆ ☆

down		
only		
way		
Down		
Only		
Way		

G	s	W	a	y	J	A	C
V	o	n	l	y	l	a	v
J	x	n	a	o	n	d	H
w	O	w	x	D	q	k	p
c	J	r	K	Z	o	o	L
Z	q	F	m	w	Z	w	X
Y	b	s	g	d	o	w	n
B	o	S	a	E	F	f	L

down   only   way

SIGHT WORD SET 40

☆ Read and trace ☆

find   use   may

☆ ☆ Color it ☆ ☆

find   use   may

☆ Circle them ☆

find
use
may

summer may use way look find

today near keep may follow

white find cold use

☆ ☆ Spell it ☆ ☆

Did you _____ it?

_____ soap and wash your hands.

I have some candy?

WORDS

☆ ☆ **Find them** ☆ ☆

find
use
may
Find
Use
May

F	N	f	m	a	y	M	v
k	i	i	g	a	F	R	o
k	j	n	M	r	D	b	x
Z	d	d	d	G	U	m	u
k	s	K	z	d	A	s	s
H	f	j	U	U	w	U	e
J	l	s	t	Q	Z	m	F
K	y	Y	p	Z	x	P	e

find

use

may

SIGHT WORD SET 41

☆ Read and trace ☆

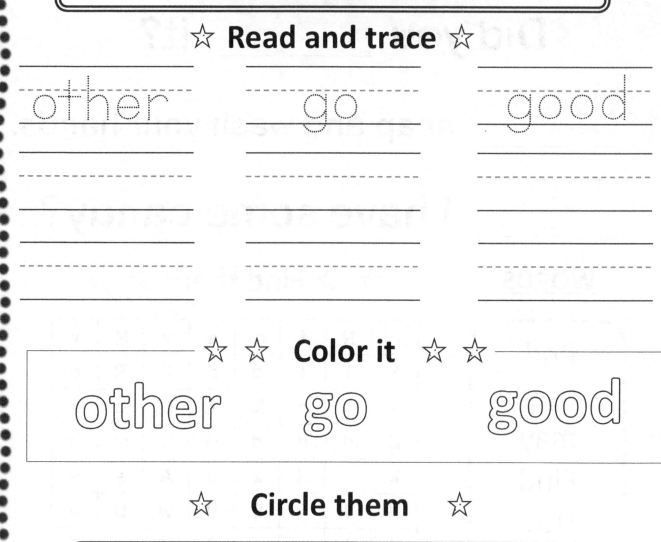

other   go   good

☆ ☆ Color it ☆ ☆

other   go   good

☆ Circle them ☆

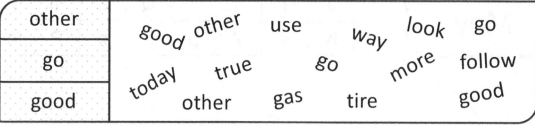

other
go
good

good other use way look go
today true go more follow
other gas tire good

☆ ☆ Spell it ☆ ☆

It is the _____ way around.

_____ outside and play.

Today is a _____ day.

WORDS

☆ ☆ Find them ☆ ☆

other
go
good
Other
Go
Good

V	l	m	V	t	E	P	R
w	z	L	E	t	L	q	U
p	A	s	J	I	L	m	I
r	o	O	t	h	e	r	m
G	g	e	t	E	e	F	k
B	o	q	X	h	W	j	b
N	c	o	t	z	o	o	D
g	o	o	d	J	b	W	d

other

go

good

SIGHT WORD SET 42

☆ Read and trace ☆

new   write   our

☆ ☆ Color it ☆ ☆

new   write   our

☆ Circle them ☆

| new |
| write |
| our |

tell bell new way write she

now true friend ball our

our write tire new

☆ ☆ Spell it ☆ ☆

I got a _____ puppy.

Can you _____ your name?

Is that _____ purple cow?

WORDS

☆ ☆ **Find them** ☆ ☆

new							
write							
our							
New							
Write							
Our							

K	n	e	w	r	i	t	e
N	p	o	O	b	i	t	x
e	n	k	u	n	i	e	z
w	h	P	r	r	E	s	K
h	T	i	W	A	R	v	b
A	O	r	X	i	c	T	l
Q	F	Z	s	Q	W	H	A
K	N	c	T	d	l	L	n

new

write

our

SIGHT WORD SET 43

used

me

man

☆ ☆ **Color it** ☆ ☆

used   me   man

☆ **Circle them** ☆

used
me
man

ring   used   pink   man   write   used

now   orange   me   ball   grass

me   short   cloud   man

☆ ☆ **Spell it** ☆ ☆

She _____ glasses to read.

Can you see _____ ?

That _____ is tall.

WORDS   ☆ ☆ **Find them** ☆ ☆

used
me
man
Used
Me
Man

w	n	T	q	m	M	F	C
p	f	J	u	s	e	d	O
u	t	N	B	Z	e	O	x
q	G	D	J	s	U	x	Y
c	B	k	U	I	L	Q	q
M	j	f	J	a	M	n	P
s	a	Y	G	m	S	T	P
m	a	n	r	J	p	J	Q

used   me   man

SIGHT WORD SET 44

☆ Read and trace ☆

☆ ☆ Color it ☆ ☆

too   any   day

☆ Circle them ☆

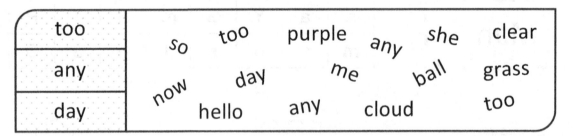

too
any
day

so   too   purple   any   she   clear

now   day   me   ball   grass

hello   any   cloud   too

☆ ☆ Spell it ☆ ☆

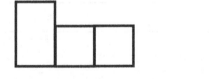  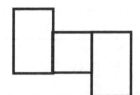

☆ **Put it in a sentence** ☆

You can come _____ .

Do you see _____ of your friends?

What a beautiful _____ !

WORDS   ☆ ☆ **Find them** ☆ ☆

too
any
day
Too
Any
Day

Q	J	O	k	r	Q	V	V
j	M	o	g	N	b	F	Z
b	O	m	l	t	y	T	z
B	C	i	Y	a	o	o	n
b	R	C	d	n	l	o	B
S	W	D	a	y	P	e	N
l	A	K	n	r	o	y	X
d	C	A	E	C	d	S	R

too   any   day

_____   _____   _____

SIGHT WORD SET 45

☆ Read and trace ☆

same   right   look

☆ ☆ Color it ☆ ☆

same   right   look

☆ Circle them ☆

same
right
look

proud   same   look   mirror   she   same

now   happy   right   ball   bug

right   any   share   look

☆ ☆ Spell it ☆ ☆

They are all the _____ .

Turn to the _____ .

_____ at him.

WORDS ☆ ☆ **Find them** ☆ ☆

same
right
look
Same
Right
Look

s	a	m	e	t	f	f	t
K	p	m	h	A	t	k	V
R	a	g	B	Q	o	Y	l
S	i	l	o	o	k	S	V
r	Q	g	L	l	h	V	k
A	r	r	h	m	B	E	r
y	a	F	c	t	s	M	j
N	y	A	O	T	x	P	j

same   right   look

SIGHT WORD SET 46

such   here   take

☆ ☆ **Color it** ☆ ☆

such   here   take

☆ **Circle them** ☆

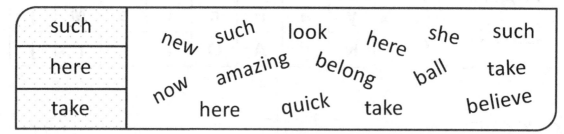

such
here
take

new   such   look   here   she   such

now   amazing   belong   ball   take

here   quick   take   believe

☆ ☆ **Spell it** ☆ ☆

 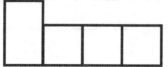 

We have _____ good friends.

_____ is your food.

_____ only what you need.

WORDS

☆ ☆ **Find them** ☆ ☆

such
here
take
Such
Here
Take

M	f	S	j	n	Q	I	T
R	d	s	T	R	S	R	Q
J	y	a	p	a	t	A	Z
O	t	W	J	r	k	T	m
S	Y	a	W	o	k	e	d
H	u	v	k	Q	r	z	h
L	s	c	H	e	r	e	m
s	u	c	h	D	J	g	U

such

here

take

SIGHT WORD SET 47

why   things   help

☆ ☆ **Color it** ☆ ☆

why   things   help

☆ **Circle them** ☆

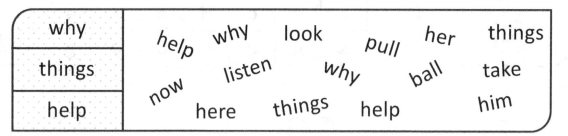

why
things
help

help why look pull her things

now listen why ball take

here things help him

☆ ☆ **Spell it** ☆ ☆

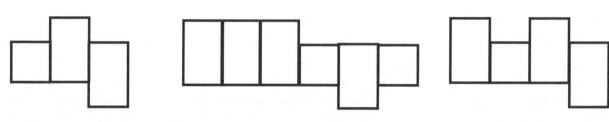

_____ do you like it?

These _____ are good for you.

Can you _____ me?

WORDS

☆ ☆ **Find them** ☆ ☆

why

things

help

Why

Things

Help

t	V	w	K	b	O	e	i
h	u	T	h	i	n	g	s
i	e	l	M	y	q	B	M
n	i	l	h	X	x	v	v
g	M	W	p	a	t	R	J
s	P	I	X	g	R	Q	K
t	e	v	C	q	F	G	F
H	L	o	b	w	c	R	y

why

things

help

SIGHT WORD SET 48

put   different   years

☆ ☆ **Color it** ☆ ☆

put   different   years

☆ **Circle them** ☆

put
different
years

bag   put   away   pull   her   years

now   years   why   different   take

different   things   yes   put

☆ ☆ **Spell it** ☆ ☆

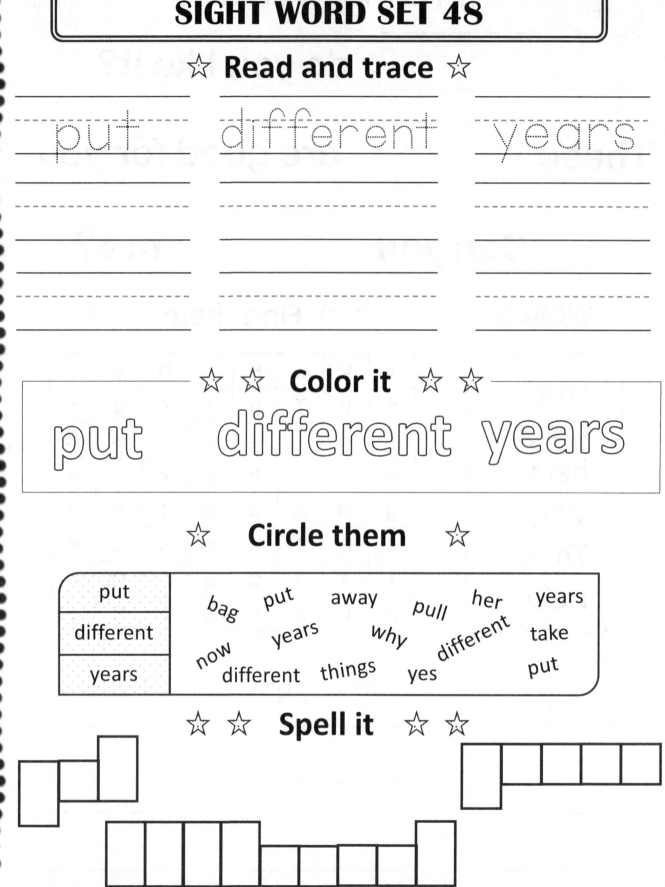

☆ Put it in a sentence ☆

Please _____ **it away.**

These are not _____ **.**

She is five _____ **older then me.**

WORDS

put
different
years
Put
Different
Years

☆ ☆ Find them ☆ ☆

D	K	R	X	J	B	P	u	t
Z	G	n	E	O	e	b	n	e
k	H	V	g	w	L	e	b	x
m	w	m	J	D	r	W	Y	h
a	c	T	Y	e	a	r	s	U
b	d	V	f	B	L	r	l	p
F	Z	f	O	l	a	E	y	u
d	i	f	f	e	r	e	n	t

put   different   years

SIGHT WORD SET 49

☆ Read and trace ☆

away   again   off

☆ ☆ Color it ☆ ☆

away   again   off

☆ Circle them ☆

| away |
| away |
| again |
| off |

away why slide again her away
now listen off roll take
again things need off

☆ ☆ Spell it ☆ ☆

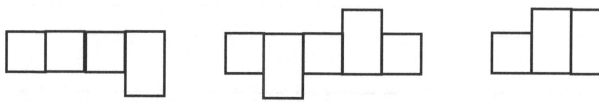

When do you go _____ ?

Can you say that _____ ?

Turn the light _____ .

WORDS   ☆ ☆ **Find them** ☆ ☆

away
again
off
Away
Again
Off

k	j	q	Z	d	G	a	T
O	c	A	g	a	i	n	e
s	d	Y	w	w	i	w	d
l	e	v	h	a	O	m	N
F	M	l	g	y	y	f	c
m	x	a	M	g	d	w	f
r	v	V	U	C	Y	f	Q
s	A	u	M	G	o	u	l

away   again   off

SIGHT WORD SET 50

☆ Read and trace ☆

went   old   number

☆ ☆ Color it ☆ ☆

went   old   number

☆ Circle them ☆

went
old
number

away went slide again went away

old toad off number few

work number chew old

☆ ☆ Spell it ☆ ☆

Do you know where she _____ ?

How _____ are you?

What's your favorite _____ ?

WORDS

☆ ☆ Find them ☆ ☆

went
old
number
Went
Old
Number

d	I	L	K	e	b	Q	M
N	m	t	k	e	c	F	J
Z	u	k	w	G	O	o	E
n	u	m	b	e	r	l	x
H	h	e	b	K	n	d	d
z	L	S	W	e	n	t	p
G	P	b	j	z	r	m	t
F	N	I	S	b	f	C	F

went   old   number

Did Enjoy This Book?

We'd love to hear your thoughts on this book.

Visit
https://sendfox.com/lp/3ez2ok

Leave this book a review and we'll send you something special.

We may even provide you with a digital copy of our next educational book.

Made in the USA
Monee, IL
26 July 2024